MLB's Greatest Teams

SAN FRANCISCO GIANTS

Katie Lajiness

Big Buddy Books
An Imprint of Abdo Publishing
abdopublishing.com

abdopublishing.com

Published by Abdo Publishing, a division of ABDO, PO Box 398166, Minneapolis, Minnesota 55439.

Printed in the United States of America, North Mankato, Minnesota.
052018
092018

THIS BOOK CONTAINS RECYCLED MATERIALS

Cover Photo: Ezra Shaw/Getty Images.
Interior Photos: 33ft/Depositphotos (p. 7); AP Images (pp. 11, 13, 19, 22, 23); Doug Pensinger/Getty Images (p. 29); Elsa/Getty Images (pp. 5, 27); Ezra Shaw/Getty Images (p. 9); Greg Trott/Getty Images (p. 17); Harry Harris/AP Images (p. 28); Jason O. Watson/Getty Images (p. 21); Jennifer Stewart/Getty Images (pp. 24, 25); Otto Greule Jr/Getty Images (p. 15); Tom DiPace/AP Images (p. 23).

Coordinating Series Editor: Tamara L. Britton
Graphic Design: Jenny Christensen

Library of Congress Control Number: 2017962674

Publisher's Cataloging-in-Publication Data

Names: Lajiness, Katie, author.
Title: San Francisco Giants / by Katie Lajiness.
Description: Minneapolis, Minnesota : Abdo Publishing, 2019. | Series: MLB's greatest teams | Includes online resources and index.
Identifiers: ISBN 9781532115196 (lib.bdg.) | ISBN 9781532155918 (ebook)
Subjects: LCSH: Major League Baseball (Organization)--Juvenile literature. | Baseball teams--United States--History--Juvenile literature. | San Francisco Giants (Baseball team)--Juvenile literature. | Sports teams--Juvenile literature.
Classification: DDC 796.35764--dc23

Contents

Major League Baseball

League Play

There are two leagues in MLB. They are the American League (AL) and the National League (NL). Each league has 15 teams and is split into three divisions. They are east, central, and west.

The San Francisco Giants is one of 30 Major League Baseball (MLB) teams. The team plays in the National League West **Division**.

Throughout the season, all MLB teams play 162 games. The season begins in April and can continue until November.

The Giants have two mascots. Fans love seeing Crazy Crab and Lou Seal *(shown)* at home games.

A Winning Team

The Giants team is from San Francisco, California. The team's colors are black, orange, and cream.

The team has had good seasons and bad. But time and again, the Giants players have proven themselves. Let's see what makes the Giants one of MLB's greatest teams!

Fast Facts

HOME FIELD: AT&T Park

TEAM COLORS: Black, orange, and cream

TEAM SONG: "Bye, Bye Baby!" by KSFO Radio

PENNANTS: 23

WORLD SERIES TITLES: 1905, 1921, 1922, 1933, 1954, 2010, 2012, 2014

CANADA
UNITED STATES OF AMERICA
MEXICO
Oregon
Nevada
San Francisco
California
Arizona
PACIFIC OCEAN
MEXICO
N
W
E
S

AT&T Park

Over the years, the Giants have played on many different fields. From 1883 to 1958, the team played near New York City, New York. Beginning in 1960, they played home games at Candlestick Park in San Francisco.

The team finally moved to its current home at AT&T Park in 2000. This ballpark seats nearly 42,000 people.

The Giants and the Los Angeles Dodgers are rivals. This rivalry began in the 1800s and continues today.

Then and Now

John B. Day and Jim Mutrie started the team in 1883. At the time, the team was called the New York Gothams. That same year, the Gothams entered the NL.

The team changed its name to the Giants in 1885. Players won their first **pennant** three years later. Then in 1888 and 1889, the team earned back-to-back World Series titles.

Owner Jim Mutrie happily described the ball players as "giants." After that, the team changed its name to the Giants.

The Giants have seen many ups and downs throughout history. The team did not finish higher than third place during the 1940s.

But in 1948, new manager Leo Durocher joined the team. He led the Giants to the World Series in 1951 and 1954.

In 1957, NL owners allowed the New York Giants to move to San Francisco. Owner Horace Stoneham thought a move would make the team stronger. However, the Giants suffered from poor playing and a loss of fans.

About 200,000 people attended a 1958 parade in San Francisco. Fans cheered about the Giants' move to the West Coast.

Highlights

Beginning in the late 1990s, the Giants began to turn losses into winning seasons. From 1997 to 2006, the team ended each season in third place or higher.

Then in 2010, the Giants played the Texas Rangers in the World Series. The Giants won four out of five games. So they took home the World Series title! That was the beginning of the team's World Series streak.

In 1997, the Giants beat the San Diego Padres 6–1 to win the NL West title.

Win or Go Home

The top team from each AL and NL division goes to the playoffs. Each league also sends one wild-card team. One team from the AL and one from the NL will win the pennant. The two pennant winners then go to the World Series!

The team's talented players have had many exciting moments on the field. In 2012, Matt Cain pitched the first **perfect game** in the team's 135-year history!

The Giants' greatest success was winning eight World Series titles. The Giants are tied for third for the team with the most World Series titles.

During the 2008 season, nearly 3 million fans attended Giants games.

Famous Managers

John McGraw was a tough manager. He played for the Giants from 1902 to 1906. And he also managed the team from 1902 to 1932.

In his 30-year **career**, McGraw earned ten NL **pennants**. And he helped the team win three World Series. In 1932, McGraw **retired** with 2,763 wins. Five years later, McGraw joined the National Baseball Hall of Fame.

McGraw managed the NL in the very first All-Star Game in 1933.

Bruce Bochy began managing the Giants in 2007. Since then, he has helped the team come back from some big losses. In 2010, he led the struggling team all the way to the World Series.

Bochy has had an 11-year **career** with the Giants. He has led the team to three World Series wins. In 2017, Bochy celebrated 900 wins as the Giants' manager.

Bochy's son Brett played with the Giants in 2014 and 2015.

Star Players

1958 – 1972

Willie Mays CENTER FIELD, #24

Willie Mays joined the New York Giants at 20 years old. He earned the 1951 **Rookie** of the Year Award his first year. Mays appeared in 24 All-Star Games. He is tied with Hank Aaron and Stan Musial for being in the most All-Star Games. To honor Mays, the team **retired** his jersey number in 1974.

Willie McCovey FIRST BASEMAN, #44

Willie McCovey earned the NL Rookie of the Year Award during his first year. Ten years later, he earned the NL **Most Valuable Player (MVP)** Award. Then he won the All-Star MVP Award and the Major League Player of the Year Award. He was a six-time All-Star participant and a three-time NL home run leader.

1959 – 1973

Juan Marichal PITCHER, #27

Pitcher Juan Marichal appeared in ten All-Star Games throughout his **career**. He earned the All-Star **MVP** Award in 1965. He also received the 1969 NL pitching title. That means that Marichal's opponents scored fewer runs while he was pitching. In 1983, Marichal joined the National Baseball Hall of Fame.

1960 – 1973

Barry Bonds OUTFIELDER, #25

1993 – 2007

Barry Bonds is one of the most well-known ballplayers in MLB. He is a seven-time NL MVP and a 14-time All-Star Game participant. Winner of eight **Gold Glove** and 12 **Silver Slugger** awards, he also holds several NL records. Bonds holds the record for most home runs in a single season. He hit 73 homers in 2001!

Madison Bumgarner PITCHER, #40

A star pitcher, Madison Bumgarner has helped the Giants win three World Series titles. In 2014, he earned the World Series **MVP** Award for excellent pitching. That year, he also won the **Babe Ruth Award** for the best performance in the **postseason**.

Buster Posey CATCHER, #28

Buster Posey showed his skills from the beginning. He won the 2010 NL **Rookie** of the Year Award. Two years later, he earned the NL MVP Award. As a 2016 **Gold Glove Award** winner, managers and coaches thought he displayed good fielding skills.

Brandon Belt FIRST BASEMAN, #9

In 2012, Brandon Belt became one of the Giants' starting first basemen. The next year, he was the NL August Player of the Week. In 2016, Belt led the Giants with 17 home runs. And, he **putout** 1,284 players during the 2016 season! Belt has been in one All-Star Game and two World Series.

Hunter Pence RIGHT FIELDER, #8

Hunter Pence was in the 2012 and 2014 World Series **championships** with the Giants. He even hit a homer in Game One of the 2014 World Series. Since Pence's **career** began, he has played in about 159 games per season. Pence won the 2013 Willie Mac Award for most inspirational player on the team.

Final Call

The Giants have a long, rich history. The team has been in 22 World Series, and it has won eight.

Even during losing seasons, true fans have stuck by the team. Many believe that the Giants will remain one of the greatest teams in MLB.

All-Stars

The best players from both leagues come together each year for the All-Star Game. This game does not count toward the regular season records. It is simply to celebrate the best players in MLB.

The Giants beat the New York Mets 3–0 in the 2016 NL Wild-Card Game.

Through the Years

1885

The New York Gothams earned a .759 winning percentage. It is still the highest winning percentage in the team's history.

1902

Manager John McGraw encouraged his entire team to learn sign language. He wanted the players to be able to communicate with a deaf player on the team.

1949

The Giants welcomed Monte Irvin and Hank Thompson to the team. They were the first two African-American players to join the Giants.

1957

The New York Giants moved to San Francisco, California.

1976

Because of low attendance at the games, the Giants considered moving to Toronto, Canada.

1989

Just before Game Three of the World Series, an earthquake struck San Francisco. The series was delayed ten days.

2002

The Giants made the league **playoffs** as a **wild-card** team. The team went on to win the NL **pennant**.

2014

Madison Bumgarner pitched to help the Giants win their third World Series title in five years.

Glossary

career a period of time spent in a certain job.

championship a game, a match, or a race held to find a first-place winner.

Babe Ruth Award given to the MLB player with the best performance in the postseason.

division a number of teams grouped together in a sport for competitive purposes.

Gold Glove Award annually given to the MLB players with the best fielding experience.

Most Valuable Player (MVP) the player who contributes the most to his or her team's success.

pennant the prize that is awarded to the champions of the two MLB leagues each year.

perfect game a baseball game in which a pitcher allows no hits, no runs, and no opposing batter to reach first base.

playoffs a game or series of games to determine a championship or to break a tie.

postseason a period of time immediately after the regular season. Teams will play against each other in a series of games to find a winner.

putout an action that causes a batter or runner on the opposite team to be out.

retire to give up one's job, or to withdraw from use or service.

rookie a player who is new to the major leagues until he meets certain criteria.

Silver Slugger Award given every year to the best offensive players in MLB.

wild-card a player or team chosen to fill a place in a competition after the regularly qualified players or teams have all been decided.

Online Resources

Booklinks NONFICTION NETWORK
FREE! ONLINE NONFICTION RESOURCES

To learn more about the San Francisco Giants, visit **abdobooklinks.com**. These links are routinely monitored and updated to provide the most current information available.

Index